How to Start a Business

"If they could do it, then you can do it too."

Author: Jimmy Bitzas

Copyright © 2023 Jimmy Bitzas.

Legal Disclaimer

All rights reserved. No part of this publication may be reproduced, distributed, or transmitted in any form by any means, including photocopying, recording, or other electronic or mechanical methods without the prior written permission of the publisher, except in the case of brief quotations embodied in critical review and certain noncommercial uses permitted by copyright law.

Neither the author nor the publisher assumes any responsibility or liability whatsoever on behalf of the consumer or reader of this material. The resources in this book are provided for informational purposes only and it should not be used to replace specialized training and professional judgment of professionals.

While we try to keep the information up-to-date and correct, there are no representations or warranties, express or implied, about the completeness, accuracy, reliability, suitability, or availability with respect to the information, products, services contained in this Book for any purpose. It is not intended to be a source of financial or legal advice. Any use of the methods describe within this Book are the author's personal thoughts. They are not intended to be a definitive set of instructions for any projects. You may discover there are other methods and materials to accomplish the same end result."

Printed In the United States

For more information, or to book an event, please contact
Jimmy Bitzas at: dbitzas@gmail.com

ISBN - Paperback: 123456789

First Edition: January 2023

Table of Contents

HOW TO START A BUSINESS 1

ABOUT THE BOOK 7

INTRODUCTION 9

MINDSET 23

TIME TO PICK 34

RESEARCH 43

EXECUTION 52

MARKETING 61

WORK LIFE BALANCE 74

CUSTOMER SERVICE 84

TECHNOLOGY 97

CONCLUSION 108

"If they could do it, then you could do it too."

Dedication

This book is dedicated to my wife Tanya. Although she may not always have agreed with what I'm doing, she gave me the freedom to live my dreams and make my own decisions when it comes to starting a business, while also standing behind me and supporting me in my endeavors. I love you for that and many other things.

Jimmy Bitzas

"If they could do it, then you could do it too."

About the Book

My name is Jimmy Bitzas, and I can honestly say I am an entrepreneur. I've started numerous businesses and been successful at many of them since I was 10 years old. I decided to write a book on becoming an entrepreneur to share what I learned along the way.

This book is more than just talking about what it takes to be successful as an entrepreneur. This book should help you decide if you are in the correct mindset to start your own business. It will ask you certain questions and help you think about the pros and cons of starting your own company. Thank you and enjoy the read.

Jimmy Bitzas

"If they could do it, then you could do it too."

Introduction

It's possible to feel overwhelmed while beginning a new business venture, but that doesn't have to be the case. To even entertain the idea of launching your own company, you need to have the correct frame of mind. You also need the willingness to put in some effort and conduct some research.

You must tell yourself that if someone else can do it, then you could do it as well. You must keep telling yourself that. This is something that I have learned over the years by starting numerous businesses and having very few failures.

First, a brief introduction of myself. I promise not to bore you with all the insignificant particulars, but first, some facts. I was born in Montreal, Canada, and later immigrated to New York. I settled in a little Town named Island Park, NY, where virtually everyone was acquainted with one another. My family moved there when I was around five years old, and neither of my parents spoke much, if any, English when we first arrived. My family did not come from a wealthy background, but I am not going to say stuff like I had to walk five miles barefoot to get to school because that is not the point I am trying to make with this discussion. My point is that if I wanted to buy something, I had to get very creative about how to make the money, and when I say creative, I don't mean stealing, selling drugs, or engaging in any other kind of illegal activity. Rather, I mean working at a very young age to try to make some extra money to buy things that my parents couldn't afford to buy for me.

When I was a kid in the late 1970s and early 1980s, my friends and I used to get excited when it snowed because it meant we could go around to our neighbors' houses and ask them if they wanted us to shovel their walkways for $5. This may not seem like a lot of money now, but it was a significant sum back then. The fact that it didn't snow every day was the

"If they could do it, then you could do it too."

main issue. Due to the influence that Mother Nature had on that business model, it was not successful for very long. The next thing that came to me was to get a paper route, just as every other kid in the area did. This plan worked out well for a while, but when it started to snow or rain, it became more difficult to maintain the route while simultaneously keeping up with my schoolwork. Therefore, that business plan was also not successful in the end.

After that, I made the decision to simply find work after school, which I ultimately did. I started out by cleaning the local food establishment that all of us kids went to for lunch. As I got older, I started pumping gas at my dad's gas station. Additionally, I started washing dishes at a local restaurant in the evening. I did everything I could to make money.

I believe that at the time, I regarded myself as successful because I was able to make money from working all these different kinds of jobs. But at the same time, I wasn't making nearly enough money to significantly alter my life. Yes, I was successful in making enough money to go on dates, see a movie, and maybe even order pizza from a restaurant.

My problem was that I needed more money but had no idea how to make it. Since everyone I knew was in the same situation as me, I did not have a mentor, nor was there anyone I could ask for assistance from.

When I turned 16, I was excited because I was finally eligible to acquire my driver's license. I had been able to save enough money performing all these jobs to afford to get my license. This was something that I had been looking forward to since I was a young child. After getting my license, I felt quite mature and desired additional responsibilities.

When the manager of the restaurant where I was working at the time found out that I had recently obtained my driver's license, he came up to me and asked me a peculiar question. At the time, I had no idea where he was going with this, so I was taken aback by his inquiry. He asked me if I could drive a

"If they could do it, then you could do it too."

car with a manual transmission. I inquired of him as to why. He informed me that he wanted me to valet for the evening and park automobiles for the guests for the evening. He went on to tell me that two valets did not show up for work, and because it was a Friday night, one of the busiest nights of the week, he was in a bind. Looking back, I think he would have asked anybody with a driver's license, but since he already had an extra dishwasher and needed a valet more than he needed a backup dishwasher, I was a good choice.

Even though I was aware that I was not the best at driving a vehicle with a manual transmission, of course I did not tell him that. I guess that at the time, I just intended to learn as I went along. I answered without hesitation, saying yes and yes. I apologize to everyone with a manual transmission who had their car parked by me. I jumped at the chance, not only for the tips, but also for the thrill of being able to drive cars that I would otherwise never be able to drive. At the time, I had the impression that I would never be able to amass enough money to purchase one of them for myself. I still remember it as if it were yesterday; it was around three o'clock in the afternoon, and the first vehicle to pull up was a large pickup truck. Of course, I acted as if I could handle the truck, even though I had to park it within inches of other vehicles. As the gentleman exited the vehicle, I dashed to the opposite side of the vehicle to open the passenger door for his female friend. I figured that was what valets did, just like in the movies. I was really delighted when the well-dressed gentleman handed me a gratuity and told me to take care of his truck. He then went on to tell me that he would take care of me as well on his way out if I did a good job and watched over it.

Then another car pulled up; I believe it was a Mercedes, and again a gentleman exited the vehicle. Once again, I opened the door for his female friend, and once again I collected a gratuity; this is when I began working as a valet. That was the beginning of my profession.

"If they could do it, then you could do it too."

I had no idea that it was going to have such a profound impact on my life at the time, but I will explain how it did. At the end of the night, I had approximately one hundred dollars in my pocket, which seemed like a life-changing amount of money to me at that moment. That evening, I naively assured myself that I could keep doing what I was doing for the rest of my life. At the close of the night, the manager came up to me and told me that he was extremely pleased with how well I had performed.

My interaction with the patrons was one of the things that left my manager impressed, and as a result, he asked me if I would be available to work the following day. It was a far more enjoyable way to make money than cleaning dishes, so I was delighted to do it again. At the end of the following night, the manager came up to me and told me that going forward, I would no longer be required to wash the dishes and that I would be able to do valet parking instead.

When I first started working as a valet, the weather

was perfect. It was the end of the summer and the beginning of October; the temperature was just right—neither too hot nor too cold. New Yorkers couldn't have asked for anything more. But, before I knew it, the chilly weather arrived—the kind where the cold air coming off the Atlantic Ocean just ripped through you. You know the kind I'm talking about, right? You have no chance of warming up under these conditions. After that, the true pain begins with the snow, specifically the process of clearing snow off other people's automobiles. I remember thinking to myself at the time that doing dishes in a toasty kitchen seemed like a nice idea. Being a valet began to put a strain on me, both physically and mentally. But what options do I have? Because I was short on cash, I decided to keep my mouth shut. When I was working at the restaurant one evening and saw car after car arrive for the dinner rush, I thought to myself, "I wonder what all of these folks do for a living." I made up my mind that I would question them about it whenever I had the chance and

"If they could do it, then you could do it too."

whenever I had the impression that they were willing to discuss and give that information.

When I asked people what they did for a living, one person said "Plumber", another person said "Painter", and yet another person said he owned a cleaning company. After hearing from salespeople, business professionals, and other people involved in various aspects of the business world, it suddenly occurred to me that most of them were business owners.

That day was the turning point in my life. One evening, I got the chance to talk to an individual who had just driven up in a Rolls Royce, of all vehicles. He got out of the car and informed me he needed a few minutes since his wife was talking on the phone in the passenger seat. Keep in mind that back then, it cost probably around a dollar per minute to talk on the phone, and not many people had cell phones. Because he was just standing there, I decided to take advantage of the situation and ask him what he did for a living.

So, I gave it a shot. He bowed his head respectfully and expressed gratitude after hearing what a gorgeous car it was. Then I asked him, "If you don't mind me asking, what do you do for a livelihood that allows you to buy such a nice vehicle?" Then I started asking him more questions. He remained silent for a while, and during that time I thought to myself, "Oh no, I may have gone too far with my questions." He then looked at me and said that he builds houses for a living. I looked at him and said, "I wish I knew how to build houses. I know nothing about building houses. I would consider it a success if I just knew how to just build a wooden box." I think that would be a great career, and obviously it appears to be a good way to make money.

He told me that twenty years ago, he would have been lucky if he knew what a hammer was. He wanted to learn how to build a house, so he obtained a job as an apprentice to a builder. He told me that

"If they could do it, then you could do it too."

everything comes back to the way you think about it. After that, he went on to say that he simply observed and learned as much as he could, and then one day he was no longer an apprentice. He had become a full-fledged carpenter with his own trainee working under him.

Then, when he thought he had learned everything he could possibly learn and after he had saved some money, he made the decision to take the plunge and establish his own company. He told me that he began his construction business with nothing more than an old pickup truck and a few tools. He began by constructing garages and sheds for customers, but he soon became so busy that he had to hire his first employee. Before he knew it, he was working on constructing his first home. He simply applied all he had learned and made it slightly better than the other companies around. According to him, he kept telling himself that if they could do it, then so could he, and the rest, as they say, is history.

I did my best to heed his counsel, but I wasn't particularly successful in school, and I had no idea what I wanted to do with my life. I wanted to launch a business but didn't want to spend a lot of money doing it. So, I decided to create a commercial cleaning company instead.

I had a limited amount of money, so I purchased a beat-up van. Unfortunately, the van caught fire, but that is a tale for another day. I was all set to start my business with just a few mops, some rags, a vacuum cleaner, and some flyers and business cards. I didn't do anything special; I just started going door to door, and wouldn't you know it, I started receiving jobs! Even though I was turned down numerous times, I did not give up.

I was determined to not only do a good job, but a fantastic job, with the gigs that I did end up getting. Then, as if by magic, news got around. I found myself with another job, then another. My company was able to expand thanks to the additional work that

"If they could do it, then you could do it too."

came in. I was able to buy two more pieces of carpet cleaning equipment and even a second truck. From there, it continued to grow. My argument is that if you have the desire to start your own business and the determination to see it through, you can succeed. The purpose of this book is to provide you with an honest explanation of what I did well and what I did poorly, and you will be responsible for deciding how to proceed from there.

Jimmy Bitzas

"If they could do it, then you could do it too."

CHAPTER 1

Mindset

If you want to be successful as an entrepreneur and read anything from this book, make it this chapter on mindset. I am putting this chapter first because this going to be the most important thing, I tell you. I believe you start here because the correct mindset is critical to starting a business. The rest of the book may give you some ideas on what to do, but the chances of you succeeding are much lower without the correct mindset.

Achieving success is significantly reliant on one's self-assurance. Individuals who always doubt themselves often cannot accomplish their aspirations as their pessimistic thoughts work as barriers, stopping them from doing the things they desire. That is why the initial stride for success in business is having a positive attitude and believing in yourself.

When you set a target, you may find that some people in your life may regard your goal as impossible or far-fetched. You may also hear a small voice inside your head telling you that you can't do what you plan to do. If you wish to prosper, you must find a way to muffle both the skeptics in your life and your pessimistic inner voice. Allowing either of them to be heard can damage your best efforts and make certain that you do not meet success. The suitable approach may differ from individual to individual. At times, friends and family may not recognize that they are being negative.

It can be difficult to evade the internal critic since you carry it with you all the time. An excellent option is to reframe the negativity and imagine that instead of being harsh on yourself, you are talking to a beloved friend. You would not be impolite or insensitive to a friend, so don't treat yourself as such either! It is easier to trust in yourself when you recognize your strengths. Everyone has their own

"If they could do it, then you could do it too."

talents, so why not appreciate them? You can foster a mindset of self-belief by making a list of your gifts. Are you great at sales? A creator? A team facilitator? Compile your strongest qualities and aptitudes and then convert them into affirmations. When going into a gathering or discussion or planning session, read the list and remind yourself that you are a superb negotiator or a proficient speaker. This will bring a bounce in your step and assist you in keeping a positive attitude.

Acknowledging one's strengths is essential, but it is just as important to tackle fears and negative thoughts. Everyone is afraid of something, but it is how we manage those fears that sets us apart. To tackle negative thoughts, try to think of what you would tell a friend in the same situation and try to rephrase them into a more positive outlook. When it comes to fears, one must confront them and find ways to equip oneself with the right tools to overcome them. For example, somebody with a fear of speaking in public can join an association that you can speak in public and receive feedback and support from the other members. When aiming for a lofty goal, one can easily become discouraged, especially when looking at other people's success. It is important to remember that everyone has their own struggles. One example is the novelist, Stephen King. One of his earliest novels, *Carrie*, was rejected by more than 30 publishers before it was finally accepted. If he'd given up, he wouldn't be one of the most famous and successful authors in the world. My point is your business will never get off the ground unless you believe in yourself. We will be talking more about mindset and things to avoid.

I didn't conduct any research for this book, and I didn't go to school for business. While I'm not opposed to either of those things, I just didn't feel they were right for me. However, I do believe that any education is better than no education at all. Now that you've taken the first step by purchasing this book, as well as presumably purchasing some other books, watching some videos on YouTube, and so on,

"If they could do it, then you could do it too."

etc., you can move on to the next step. You undoubtedly still believe that you are ready to launch your own company, which is fantastic, but the real question is: are you truly ready? Or are you just trying to convince yourself that you are? Even if you feel like it's the right time, if you're considering going into business for yourself, one piece of advice I can give you is to avoid soliciting advice from close relatives and friends.

If you ask relatives and friends their opinion on whether you should start a business, that feedback will impact your decision since they are close to you. There is a chance that if you receive any negative feedback, you will convince yourself that it is not the right time to do it. This is because, in the early stages, when you are just thinking about starting a business, it's easy to back away from an idea. Think about the fact that the only person who can tell you when you're ready is yourself.

It's possible that what I'm about to say will come

across as harsh, but as I mentioned at the beginning of this book, I'm going to give you my sincere opinion and advice on how to succeed. Now, you might be thinking to yourself, "Wow, does this guy really think I could start a business without first talking to my wife or husband or my significant other?" and you'd be right to question whether I am being realistic.

Set the foundation first without any outside influences of any kind; decide first if you even want to start a business in the first place and that you feel ready to do so. I'm not saying that you should never talk to them about starting a business. What I am saying is that you should lay the foundation first. The next step is to decide what kind of company you want to launch, conduct some research on that company. View some relevant videos on YouTube, peruse print publications if they are readily available, and read some books about the kind of company you intend to launch.

The next step is to consider if you still want to launch

"If they could do it, then you could do it too."

that kind of business. If the answer is still yes, it's time to evaluate whether it's possible for you to do so financially. Ask yourself if you have the time to devote to it as well as what challenges you would need to overcome in order to succeed.

Therefore, if you can get over all those things and still feel positive about it after weighing all the benefits and drawbacks, you should go for it. Now would be a good time to sit down with your significant other and discuss your intentions with them.

You should keep in mind that up to this point, it has not cost you any money, other than perhaps the expense of acquiring some books on the topic. You are now ready to move forward with this project, if you and your significant other have agreed to do so, and you have the support you need from them.

Keep in mind that this is still in the early stages, and I strongly recommend that you still not talk to anybody else about your ideas. This is not because you should be worried about somebody stealing your idea. It is because you don't have much invested in this other than some research. It is best to keep your ideas to yourself until this process is further along. My thinking behind this is that if someone starts talking negatively about the business idea you want to start, they may convince you not to move forward with your concept, which would mean that it never had a chance to succeed in the first place.

Another piece of advice I have is to get in touch with a few individuals who run businesses like the one you want to launch. Keep in mind that you have not yet fully decided it is the type of business that you wish to launch; you are only considering the possibility. In the following chapter, we will delve deeper into the process of selecting a business. Make sure you talk to people who won't consider you a threat, and if your company is one that provides a service, try reaching out to people who live outside the area that you are aiming to provide service in. I would also recommend that you join Facebook groups that are related to your business. Over the course of my experience, I've

"If they could do it, then you could do it too."

discovered that there is a group for practically everything. After you have joined, all you need to do is pay attention to everything, both positive and negative. Take as much information away from it as you can, particularly from those who have been participating in the field for some time.

Because they have nothing to gain or lose from their recommendations, I place a considerably higher importance on the opinions of complete strangers who work in the industry that I want to break into. They have been there and can speak to both the positives and negatives of the experience. Some of them will be pessimistic because that's just how they are, but you need to weed out these people so you can focus on talking to those who are realistic and have a well-rounded view of the sector, including both its good and bad points.

Believe me when I say that you can find people who are willing to talk to you and assist you. When I launch a new company, I make it a point to consult with industry veterans who have been in the game for some time. I start by reading the evaluations other customers have left for the company, as this gives me a better idea of who they are and how other people feel about them. I then give them a call and explain to them right away who I am and what it is that I am attempting to accomplish. I also reassure them that I will not be one of their competitors, and after hearing that, most of the time the barrier between us is broken down and they are willing to chat. Inquire with them whether this is an appropriate time to speak. You always have the option of sending them an email if you have access to one, in which case you can convey the same information and watch for a response from them. Calling them rather than sending them an email has always been more successful for me. You are going to be pleasantly surprised to find out that there are more individuals wanting to chat with you than there are who would not.

"If they could do it, then you could do it too."

We just finished talking about how you should ask yourself if you still want to do it now that you've completed everything. Are you prepared to go for it? If you have the impression that the answer is yes, then you should be congratulated! You are one step closer to joining the club of genuine business owners.

CHAPTER 2

Time To Pick

It is time to choose a business now that you have done some introspection and determined that you do want to be an entrepreneur. This step may sound simple, but it is rather challenging. Because there are many different considerations to make, selecting the best idea for a business venture requires that you take your time.

You, too, could do what everyone else does and just Google "business ideas" to find a list of hundreds of potential enterprises. But before you start Googling, you need to ask yourself if you want to start a service-based business in which you travel to the customer, or if you want to start a work-from-home kind of business in which you don't have to leave your house, or if you want to open a location in which customers come to you.

"If they could do it, then you could do it too."

This is the first thing you need to decide. If you want to start a work-from-home kind of business, you don't have to leave and makes things a little easier. The second thing you need to do is ask yourself if you would love doing it and if you would look forward to getting up in the morning and performing that profession. If the answer to either of those questions is no, then you need to keep looking for a business that you will be happy doing. If you are only considering the financial opportunity of the business, then I would advise you to steer clear of it. As time goes on, you will grow to hate it, and eventually you will quit. You need to be able to say that you enjoy the work that you do for a living.

Another question that you need to pose to yourself is, "Is there enough money in it to afford you the lifestyle that you would like?" For instance, you may have a strong affinity for dogs and the ambition to start a career as a dog walker. While this is an admirable goal, it is important to note that if you desire a large house on a beach, you probably won't be able to afford it with the money you get from walking dogs. I'm not saying it's impossible; I'm saying it would be very hard.

Another question you need to ask yourself is, "What are the initial costs going to be?" Do you think you will be able to start this business without putting yourself under so much financial strain that you won't be able to sleep at night? Once you start getting stressed over money and getting anxious about starting a business, it could be a path toward failure. So really think about the money factor when starting your new venture.

You should use Google at this point to find out how much money people in that profession often make. Even though it is not the most reliable source of information, it will provide you with some insight. You need to ask yourself if your company will suffer if there is a downturn in the economy, and if the answer is yes, you may want to think about switching careers because you have no influence over how the

"If they could do it, then you could do it too."

economy will turn.

When launching a business, additional questions to ask yourself include: will this be a seasonal business? If it is that is fine, just ask yourself if you will make enough money to survive in the off season.

You might investigate the profession you're thinking about entering and discover that there is a lot of competition. If this is the case, you might tell yourself, "Well, I'm not going to do that because there is too much competition." However, you should tell yourself the opposite: if there is a lot of competition, it means that the service or business you're thinking of starting is in demand.

When starting a business in an industry with a lot of competition, all you need to do is research what the major players are doing in the field, then do what they are doing but better. Always keep in mind that if they were able to succeed, you will be able to succeed as well.

My most recent foray into the business world was becoming a home inspector. I got the idea for this business from a friend who was in the process of purchasing a home. Once they had an agreement in place, the next step was to get a home inspection done. After making several phone calls, the earliest that someone could come out and perform a home inspection for him was going to be more than a week away, and it was at that moment that an idea came to me. I did my homework and asked every question I could think of, and in the end, I decided to become a home inspector. Since then, my career has been quite successful.

You might be thinking, "Well, what about if there's a downturn in the economy and people stop buying houses?" This is an understandable question. After giving it some thought, I realized that one of the advantages of working as a home inspector is that you can grow your business by offering additional services, such as energy audits, insurance inspections, pool inspections, annual home

"If they could do it, then you could do it too."

maintenance inspections, and so on. Consequently, in the grand scheme of things, even if there is a downturn in the economy, I would still be okay. My point is that when you choose a business, you should make sure that you can add services even if demand for certain of those services decreases while you are still in the same business.

The other thing that I always do is just something simple out of habit: whenever I'm driving around and see a vehicle with any kind of advertisement, I read the advertisement, and then I ask myself if I can see myself doing what they are doing for a living. Do the same thing, because once you start looking, you won't believe how many different industries you will see just by going about your day-to-day life. I highly encourage you to follow this recommendation. I also advocate using the same procedure with traditional stores made of brick and mortar.

You should also investigate the many groups on Facebook and other social media platforms to find out what people do for a living. You will be amazed by the information you uncover.

Another question that I usually ask myself is, "What type of license, if any, do I need?" since you need to keep that in mind. I'm not suggesting that getting the license would be difficult, but it is something that you need to take into consideration. As a side note, if you are thinking of starting a business that requires a lot of physical labor, you should ask yourself if you can carry out the duties that would be expected of you physically.

If you are considering moving more toward a service-based business in which you must drive to the customer's location, the first question you should ask yourself is, "Do I have the suitable vehicle for that job?" Because this might be a very expensive outlay of cash on your part. I simply want you to take into consideration the many different aspects involved in selecting the appropriate business idea.

You might be saying to yourself, "Well, all the things

"If they could do it, then you could do it too."

you're saying are common sense". They might be, but the truth is that I've seen a lot of people start businesses without thinking it all the way through. It may take you a week, four weeks, or even six months to pick and decide what it is that you want to do for a living, since it is important to take your time when making this decision. I find that going for a walk or riding my bike helps me clear my head and focus on what I want to think about. Do yourself a favor and do not rush this.

Consequently, whether you are choosing a business or a job, you should make sure that you have the impression that you will enjoy getting up in the morning and engaging in that endeavor. Look into the demand for the things you are considering doing as well, because regardless of how much you enjoy doing something, if there is very little need for it, it will just be something you do temporarily.

Jimmy Bitzas

"If they could do it, then you could do it too."

CHAPTER 3

Research

If you've decided that starting a business is what you want to do, then congrats; the fun part begins now. Do some research; at this point, it's time to start figuring out the specifics of launching this company. You're going to want to start out simply, so you can Google people or businesses that are in the same business that you want to start. Google is going to become your closest friend at this point in the process. First, you should jot down between five to ten of them.

Now go to their websites and look at all the services and products that they sell. Ask yourself if you think you can compete with what you see there. The next step that I would recommend taking is to look at all their reviews, read them all, and look at the positive ones as well as the bad ones. Then, question yourself once more if you could do better than what other people are saying about them.

Pay close attention to what people are criticizing and know that you will need to come up with a plan to make sure you don't get the same kind of bad comments.

The next thing that I would do is look at their domain names, and I have discovered that the best tool for this is the "WhoIs" tool on GoDaddy. If you use this tool, you can look up who owns the domain name and how long they have owned it. This will give you a pretty good idea of how long they have been in business. Another useful tool is going to the website of the state that they are in to find out when they became a company.

Why is this important? Because once you determine who has been in business for a while, you know that they must be doing something well. These are the businesses that you need to do additional research on in order to get a deeper understanding of all the

"If they could do it, then you could do it too."

services and goods that they provide.

After researching those businesses, you should consider whether you need to make any additional investments. Maybe you'll need additional equipment or products or to obtain additional licenses in order to compete. At the end of the day, you're going to have to match everything that the competition is doing and then do it better. You could choose to provide fewer services or products, but in that case, you will need to devise a strategy to demonstrate to clients why they should work with you rather than a competitor that has been in business for a lengthy time. Please keep in mind that cost is not the only consideration.

You are going to need to know who your ideal consumer is at the end of the day and how to capture their attention. You need to differentiate yourself from organizations that have been in business for a longer period of time.

Do not become disheartened; this is the exciting part

of the process. I enjoy competing against the larger players in the industry. When your company is just starting out, you can provide a level of personalized service that customers appreciate. Typically, they do not receive that from the larger companies. The last step that I would do is to investigate whether there are any periodicals or Facebook pages devoted to the industry, as well as any associations that I might be able to join and investigate.

It is very important to understand the mentality of individuals who work in your sector. By this, I mean that you need to comprehend the things that bother people in your field as well as the things that bring them pleasure.

At the end of the day, people like talking about themselves and their businesses. In the beginning, you should just listen, and once you feel more comfortable with the industry by understanding the fundamentals of how everything works, you should start asking questions in places like Facebook groups.

"If they could do it, then you could do it too."

Example, I joined many groups of home inspectors, and I asked lots of question after I had the basic understanding of the industry, I did run into a few idiots who said something stupid, and I did not let them discourage me. Keep in mind that one of the most important aspects of running a successful business is having the right mindset and doing everything in your power to avoid losing that.

YouTube is yet another excellent resource for gaining knowledge about the business world. Be mindful of the content: the information that can be gleaned from it may not be the most accurate. However, it is free, and users can watch videos on their own time while reading both positive and negative feedback left by other users. On YouTube, exercise caution and don't take everything to heart because no one fact-checks anything individuals say. You can still obtain some valuable information about the topic if you look for it.

Another thing that I usually look for in an industry is

trade events. These exhibits might not be in your area, and you might have to drive or fly to get to them. In my opinion, it is well worth the effort and the time you put into attending them. Where else can you get that many people in the same industry be in the same place at the same time? You never know when you might run into, maybe even someone who will become your future mentor. People that attend tradeshows are very talkative, and this is especially true when you're sitting at the bar with a group of industry professionals. If you do not take this additional step, you will find that it is much more difficult to learn a significant amount of information.

Just like when you were first considering starting a business, now is the time to talk to people who have been doing it for a while. Just like when you were first considering starting a business, I always call companies or people who are not in my marketplace, and I am always honest with them and tell them that I am getting into the industry, and if they have a few minutes to talk, I would appreciate it. Now that

"If they could do it, then you could do it too."

you've done everything mentioned above and you believe you have a basic understanding of the business.

As I mentioned before, I will start by sending out an email in which I will explain my goals and ask the recipients if it is okay to call them and, if so, when would be the most convenient time? You won't believe it, but for every five emails I send out, I receive one or two responses from people who don't feel threatened by me because I am not competing with them in their market.

It's possible that you've been telling yourself things like, "Well, Jimmy, I need to talk to people in my marketplace because what I'm starting is marketplace-driven, and other markets may not be the same." Yes, that is possible; but if you call people in your market who are going to be your future competitors, they may not be willing to talk to you.

If they are being critical, it is most likely because they are aware that you will be one of their main competitors. When communicating with people who are not part of your target market, the fundamentals will remain the same.

The entirety of this procedure could take a couple of weeks, but it is very significant since, up until this point, you have spent very little money maybe on some books and you have a strong basic idea of what you are getting yourself into, including the positives and the negatives.

You've probably heard the old saying that you don't need to reinvent the wheel; instead, you should simply find the person who is the most successful and follow their lead. This is because, with the advent of the Internet, it's easier than ever to comprehend what it is that successful people are doing.

In later chapters of this book, we will discuss how to execute this process more effectively. Do not rush through this step. You are going to be gathering a lot of information from a lot of different sources. You are probably going to get answers that conflict with each

"If they could do it, then you could do it too."

other to the questions you have. You will need to sort the information to determine what is true and what is not.

CHAPTER 4

Execution

When launching a business, execution is another crucial component to consider. Writing a business plan is the first thing that I do whenever I start a new venture. I'm not suggesting that you go crazy with this step because you can easily find examples of company business plans online that are fifty pages long, but that is not what I am referring to. There might be some advantages to doing that, but in most cases, it will not be of any assistance.

I was the one who did that. I would look up business plan templates on Google that I could follow. However, I discovered that no matter how many times I tried to utilize the ones I found, they never worked out since plans changed along the way. In the end, I just wasted a lot of time doing it. Time

"If they could do it, then you could do it too."

management is crucial in the first four weeks, those are the ones I'm focusing on when it comes to execution.

When it comes to startup cost, I always like to pad the funds by at least 10% more than the startup costs. You never know what you might run into, and if you don't use the extra 10%, good for you. The next thing I do is look at my finances and make sure that I have the funds to start the business in the first place.

If you don't have the money to start the business, then you shouldn't start it. It is my strong recommendation that you do not use credit cards. Because then, if you start a business with a credit card, you are starting out in a stressful position. If you don't make money right away, it could affect you financially, and when that happens, your thinking is thrown out the window. I also don't recommend borrowing money unless it's from a financial institution, such as a bank, with fixed terms so you can properly budget for things like a car or expensive tools. Borrowing money from a member of your family will always come back to bite you in the rear end, in my opinion.

Now, choose a location for your business. If it's a home-based enterprise, this step will be much simpler for you. If you're not sure you pick a location that you can afford. Think about everything from utilities to insurance to even your commute. How long does it take you to get there? If you need to rent the place or even buy a place. I don't recommend buying at the beginning: always rent first to make sure things work out the way you planned. If you do end up buying or renting a place, is there sufficient parking for customers who come to you? This is another subject I could write an entire chapter devoted solely to this topic.

The next step that I take is to select a business structure, such as a DBA, which stands for "doing business as". I strongly advise against doing this since you will not be protected from legal action over

"If they could do it, then you could do it too."

your personal property. Instead, you should consider forming an LLC or a corporation because these legal structures offer many benefits and are a better option overall. I am not an accountant, a CPA, or a financial advisor, so I strongly suggest that you discuss your case with either your accountant or your financial advisor. They will be able to assist you in selecting a structure that will work best for you.

Now that you picked a company structure, it's time to pick a name. Some people believe that naming your company is unimportant, but I disagree. The first thing I do is make sure that the business I'm doing is in the name. For example, if I'm a plumber, I would call it something like XYZ Plumbing Company, and if I'm an accountant, I would say something like XYZ Accounting Services. A name for your company is important.

Why should you care about this? The words in your name are probably the most important SEO factor. They say what you do, and it will help your business show up in internet search results. In case you don't know what SEO stands for, it stands for "search engine optimization". We'll go over this topic in more detail in the chapter on marketing. When deciding on a name, checking to see if the domain is available is yet another incredibly crucial consideration. That is something you can achieve by using a service like GoDaddy or Register.com. Google the name before settling on it, since the last thing you want to do is select a name for your website for which someone else already holds the domain name or close to the name you are picking. You should go for a domain name that ends in ".com." It shouldn't be a .net or anything else along those lines. Why should we care about this? Because it is one of the original domain endings, so it gives the appearance you have been around for a long time. It may sound silly, but it's not: if you can't get the .com, then you shouldn't use that name. On the other hand, if you have the possibility to get that name you want along with a .com, then yes, I propose you also purchase the

"If they could do it, then you could do it too."

second most significant one, which is the .net. It's not the end of the world if you can't acquire the second one but achieving that has always been one of my primary objectives.

After you have completed all those steps, the next step is to obtain a tax identification number from both the federal government and your state, and then register your business with both the state and, if necessary, the local business authorities in your area. Submit applications for any licenses and permits that could be required to operate the new company you've decided to launch. After you have completed all these steps, you should then proceed to open a bank account. Be aware that in order to do so for a business account, you will be required to provide proof that your firm has been registered.

When creating a checking account for your company, it is also a good idea to inquire with the bank about the possibility of obtaining a credit card or debit card in the name of the company. Do not make this an afterthought; if you do, you will be scrambling at the end of the year to try to figure out where you spent money for your business, and it will become a nightmare for you.

This is also a great time to decide what kind of accounting software you want to use to keep track of all your expenses, including mileage if you are traveling. You will want to know where every dollar goes as soon as you start your business. I use QuickBooks, but there are many other software programs available. Input all your receipts or scan them and save them in case you need them in the future. There are many programs available in the app stores on your phone that can assist you with this, and it is well worth the investment.

Again: I strongly suggest that you inquire about getting a credit or debit card from your bank. Doing so provides you with an additional simple way to keep tabs on all your expenditures. Use that one credit card for everything that relates to your

"If they could do it, then you could do it too."

company, but do not use it for anything else.

Jimmy Bitzas

"If they could do it, then you could do it too."

CHAPTER 5

Marketing

Because I enjoy marketing so much, it is probably one of the aspects of starting a new business that I enjoy the most. I enjoy starting with a clean slate. When I start a business, I do not have anything. Not a website, a marketing plan, or anything else. As a result, I look at those individuals and companies that already have those things.

I use Google to look up people and companies that are already established in the sector I want to enter. I check to see if the entities I am investigating have been operational for at least four years.

I want to make sure they have a lot of reviews and backlinks. I'll explain what those are later in this book if you're not familiar with them.

I review their websites and examine all the content that is available there. I consider the most successful companies to eventually be my rivals.

When researching your competitors, it is imperative that you analyze everything they are doing from a marketing standpoint. Try to establish benchmarks for everything that your competitors are doing. This includes all the keywords that they use on their websites, since keywords are a component of SEO, along with backlinks and a great deal of other topics, which we will touch on in this chapter.

When developing a strategy, one of the first things you should do is decide how you want to go about marketing your product or service. Depending on what you're doing with your marketing, it might be an expensive endeavor. You should consider your return on investment. However, there are specific requirements that you must meet.

Putting together a website should be one of the first things on your to-do list. I am referring to a fantastic

"If they could do it, then you could do it too."

website, not one of those sites that you create yourself that looks amateurish and unprofessional. You need one that has a professional appearance and gives the impression that your company is well established. Do not attempt to build your own website if you do not have experience in this field. I know that you might be tempted to make your own website, but it really is worth looking for a professional to complete this step.

If someone lands on your webpage, you only have a few seconds to convince them that you are the right company for them. If your website looks unprofessional, they will click off as quickly as they clicked on. This is one of the primary reasons why you should not create your own website.

It is vital that your site be SEO friendly. When a user types "car wash near me" into the search bar, if your site is not optimized for car washes in the town or city that the user was in when they performed the search, they will not see your website. If you only show up on page 3, you might as well be on page 500, so you absolutely need to invest in effective SEO for your company.

Without considering SEO, it is possible to have the most attractive website in the area and have no potential clients.

Although there are many factors that contribute to the success of a website, I will only discuss a few of them here for the time being. The reason for this is at the end of the day if you do hire someone you can make sure they followed the basic rules.

The load speed of a website is one of the factors that Google considers when determining a website's ranking. This refers to the amount of time it takes for a website to fully load on a user's device after they click on the page. Also, if you have a significant number of links that are broken. That means it's a big no-no in Google's book if visitors to your site click on a link and are taken to a page that just states there was an issue.

"If they could do it, then you could do it too."

Is it simple to find one's way around your website? You absolutely must check that your website is appears correctly on mobile devices, tablets, and personal computers, and that's just naming a few of the most critical aspects.

If you make it challenging for a customer to use your website, that customer will not use your service. In the end, when it comes to a website, you should look at everything that your competitors have on their websites, try to mix the components that are the finest from each of their websites, and then add your own personal touch.

Put together all the information for your website, including photos, and check to be sure that they are original photographs that you own. Do not download photos from the Internet or purchase them from sites like I Stock or others. If you can take your own photos that would be the best option. Once you have all that information, have a professional put it together; in most cases, you will be able to do so for less than one thousand dollars.

Both fiver.com and upwork.com are excellent venues to search for people that can assist you with your website in some way.

I could go on and on about websites; in fact, I could write an entire book about websites on their own; however, that is not the subject of this book. In the end, it is best to hire a professional rather than try to save a few dollars by building your own website, because you might come to regret it.

The following step that I would take is to remind you of something I said at the beginning of the book: "Don't tell anyone about your business". Because your website is up, and your business is ready to go, now is a good time to let everyone know about your new business. Scream it from the rooftops, tell your neighbors, coworkers, and extended family, everyone you know, and even people you don't know. Send out links to your newly finished website and ask people if they know anyone who could benefit from your

"If they could do it, then you could do it too."

services. Since you just finished your website, this is the time when you want to get social media going, from Facebook to LinkedIn to Twitter. As you probably already know, these days everyone is using social media to communicate with one another. Not only do I have a personal Facebook page, but I also have a Facebook page for my business. In the beginning, you should begin publishing two to three times a week; this will assist you in appearing in front of potential customers. We will discuss this topic in more detail later.

The next step that you need to take is to claim your online company listing in Google. If you run a service-based company, having a Google business page as well as a Bing business page will increase the likelihood that your company will appear in web searches. If you run a business out of your house, you should take this into consideration. Now that you have a website, a presence on social media, and have claimed your business, it is time to start networking. Although this topic might be the subject of an entire chapter on its own just like some other subjects in this book, I will only briefly touch on it here. Join the Chamber of Commerce together with other community groups and business associations. Facebook groups are great ways to spread awareness of your brand and let people know what you do for a living. Request that your relatives and friends "thumbs up" your Facebook page and urge them to share it with their friends. Join online communities such as nextdoor.com. Register with as many free listing services as you can, for instance. Better Business Bureau Yelp, Angie's list. I could go on and on, but I think you get the point.

You should have printed business cards as well as an electronic card that you can send or email to people. You should do anything and everything in your power to get your name out there, such as creating a QR code with all your contact information for people to scan. Create a blog and do a YouTube video. You merely want to raise people's awareness of your brand. People might not remember your brand after

"If they could do it, then you could do it too."

only one post on a social media platform, but you should keep publishing anyhow. Believe me, after they have seen it ten times and need your service, they will remember who you are.

You're going to be spending a lot of time marketing in the beginning, but trust me, that's only the beginning. Once you've established yourself and started receiving reviews, you're going to start getting referrals, and you won't have to spend as much time marketing as you did in the beginning.

Let's talk about reviews. Reviews come from hundreds of different platforms and are perhaps the most significant component of marketing. You want to gather reviews, but you want to do so in a strategic way.

One of the most common mistakes is that I see is people make it way too easy for people to leave them a review. I've noticed that some people are adding a QR code with the phrase "Give me a review" to the back of their business cards. Or they include a link on their website that allows customers to submit feedback.

You may believe that you are the best at what you do, but the fact of the matter is that you will always come across somebody who is unhappy; it's just human nature. If you run into this person on a bad day and you make it too easy for them to leave you a review, there is a chance that you will get a negative review, even if it's not your fault, and even one or two negative reviews could put you at a disadvantage.

Someone I know did that, and as a result, they ended up getting a lot of negative feedback. This was not because people were unhappy with the quality of their service; rather, it was because people were upset about something that was out of the person's control. They took out their frustration on him, and as a result, he received some negative feedback from customers he had never worked with or even heard of before. It is possible to get rid of those negative reviews but doing so can be very challenging at times.

"If they could do it, then you could do it too."

Because of this, you shouldn't make it easy for customers to provide feedback on your business.

When it comes to deciding who writes a review for you, you should exercise extreme discretion. After you have a face-to-face meeting with the customer, you can get a sense of how satisfied they are with the work you have done by simply asking them. When you are satisfied with how things are going, you should ask the customer to leave you a review. Now is the time to make it simple for people to leave you a review. Provide them with a link that can be clicked on or a QR code so that they can easily do so.

Because it is so crucial to be very selective about who you ask for a review, I have two different sets of business cards, one of which includes a QR code and the other of which does not. Most of the time, the only people who will leave reviews without being specifically asked for them are those who are upset. Satisfied customers may not leave a review without being asked. On the other side, if someone is mad at you or feels you did something wrong, even though it's not your fault, they may leave a negative review simply to lash out. People are aware that writing negative reviews is the most effective technique to hurt your business. It's all done on emotion, and typically right in the beginning when they're angry. So, make it easy for good reviews to be posted, but don't help the unsatisfied customers air their grievances.

"If they could do it, then you could do it too."

CHAPTER 6

Work Life Balance

If you want to launch your own company, you should be prepared to devote a significant amount of time to its launch, which may detract from other aspects of your life that you enjoy. After you have established the principles of your company, it is imperative that you also pay attention to the fundamentals of your personal life and the lives of your family. If you don't, the path you thought would lead you to independence and freedom may instead take you in the opposite direction.

Why did you decide to launch your own company in the first place? This is the question you need to keep asking yourself repeatedly. The most common responses I get are along the lines of "independence," "I can make my own schedule," "I don't have a boss,"

"If they could do it, then you could do it too."

and "the potential for making money could be endless." These are all valid points, but if you let your business take over your life, you will lose the ability to create your own schedule, and as a result, you will lose your independence. Therefore, if you do not strike a healthy balance between your professional and personal life, all the motivations that drove you to launch the company in the first place will evaporate, and your personal life will suffer as a result.

Don't buy into the myth that most people must be at work from Monday to Friday. This is not the turn of the century when Henry Ford was using an assembly line to make Model T automobiles. The working day doesn't have to run from 9:00 a.m. to 5:00 p.m. with only the weekend reserved for leisure activities. You must break out of the mentality that you have to work five out of the seven days of the week and that the other two days may be spent doing whatever you like. I've never really understood why people do it. Perhaps it's because our parents taught it to us, and our parents presumably learned it from our ancestors. It really doesn't matter what kind of business you decide to launch if you can meet your objectives. Your goal should be to generate the necessary revenue and achieve whatever it is you set out to do, but at the same time have a happy personal life.

If you are doing something that you enjoy and then you are on the right track. If you do not forget about your family, children, or significant other, then work can also be fun.

When I'm looking to start a new business, one of the most important questions I ask myself is, "Will this be a location-based business?" Do I need to make sure that the store is open for business at a specific hour? I did start a business that was situated in a physical location, and every day, we would go there at 8:00 AM to open the door and stay there until 6:00 PM to close it. What ended up happening was that we lost our independence, and as time went on, I started

"If they could do it, then you could do it too."

to feel resentment against the company that I had desired so much.

You are probably asking yourself right now, "Why don't you just hire someone to help you out with this problem?" That is far simpler to say than it is to accomplish. We did end up hiring someone, and everything ran smoothly for the first several weeks afterward, but then the new employee started calling in sick, opening the store late, or something broke that they were unable to fix. It seemed like there was always something going on, and at the end of the day I still had to go in—maybe not as much as before, but still enough that it was difficult for me to make plans, go on vacation, or work remotely. After running all the numbers, the outcome was not what we expected. Because of payroll and all the federal taxes (FICA, Social Security, insurance, etc.), we ended up making less money than we had anticipated.

But despite that, we were still able to make some money, and I thought to myself well, I still had some freedom, so that's okay. The subsequent quarter's sales were not as good as the first quarters. As a result, after accounting for payroll, we ended up losing money. I had to put in more hours myself while reducing the number of hours my employee put in.

After I reduced the hours of my full-time employee because I could not afford for him to be full time, he quit. I found myself in the same position as before: where I was losing my freedom. Hiring someone else may not be as easy as you think, especially if you are limited on what you can pay someone. This is the point I want to make regarding this topic: if you are planning to create a location-based business, you really need to think about it. Always keep in mind that the only person who will be fully committed to your business succeeding is yourself. After all, it's your baby, not theirs.

Because of this, going forward, I have made the decision to never create a business that will result in

"If they could do it, then you could do it too."

me losing my independence again. I won't establish a business until I have completed say over the hours I put in and the days of the week I'm required to work. When I get up in the morning, what time I want to start working, and when I want the day to end are the most important factors for me to consider when choosing my next business opportunity.

The other thing that I will make sure I will be able to do is hire a third parties to take care of things for me, from SEO to website maintenance to marketing, pretty much everything I can except answering the phone. Even though I could do all those things myself, I looked at the pros and cons of hiring those services out and concluded that my free time is more important to me than those tasks.

To achieve success, one cannot rely solely on themselves. It is understandable to be tempted to handle all aspects of the project to save money, but in the long run it will take away more time and energy than hiring extra help. You may have many skills and be great at innovating and communicating, but the reality is that nobody is equally proficient at everything. Trying to do the things you are not so great at may lead to an unsatisfactory outcome. Many entrepreneurs attempt to do it all at the start of a project, but once it is established, it would be smart to bring in assistance. That way, you will be able to focus more on the tasks that only you can do, as well as have a better quality of life, which is an essential part of being successful.

If there is a project that needs to be done, I will check to see if a third-party company can do it and get a price quote for it. After that, I will put a time frame on it and decide whether I should do it myself or see if it's worth having someone else do it. Using services that are available on websites such as fiver.com and upwork.com are good ways to maintain control over your time.

I almost always go through a third party to free up some of my time so that I can focus on operating my

"If they could do it, then you could do it too."

business and enjoying my life. Do not let anyone in your family, your friends, or anyone else tell you when you should work and when you should not work. Yes, most of the time you want off on the weekends because the kids are out of school and your significant other could be home for many different reasons. Just make your own schedule and leave plenty of time for yourself and your family while still maintaining the professionalism of your business. Do not let yourself get caught up in the rat race, as most people do.

For instance, whenever I schedule an appointment, I always make sure that it is not before 10:00 AM. This is not because I don't wake up early; rather, it is because I don't want to waste valuable time sitting in traffic every morning and joining the rat race. Consider the fact that even if you cut your travel time by only one hour each day, it amounts to hundreds of hours over the course of a year. Therefore, at the end of the day, you should make sure that you choose a business that you will like making money at and that will provide you the freedom to have the personal life that you have always desired.

"If they could do it, then you could do it too."

CHAPTER 7

Customer Service

Because providing good service to customers is so vital, I have decided to devote an entire chapter to this alone.

Your customers are the crucial element to the success of your business. If they are not content with the product or services, it will result in failure. It is as basic as that. It does not matter what the critiques of your company or product are. If your clients are pleased and fulfilled, you will make money. A customer's journey with your business begins from the time they first become aware of your brand and services and carries on as long as they utilize your products or service. While thinking about the customer experience, consider each step of the process. Give superior content, a straightforward

"If they could do it, then you could do it too."

buying process, and outstanding support. Customers who have been provided with first-class assistance will remember it, and they will bring it up to their acquaintances. Before anyone spends their money on your product or service, they will want to ensure that it will meet its pledges. You can make them feel more confident in that by giving them clear value even prior to them buying. People look up to authority figures. You can demonstrate your expertise by doing what we just discussed – providing value.

In any field you enter, regardless of the business, your reputation is the most important factor. A referral for a new client is the most lucrative type of lead that you can acquire for a potential customer from an existing customer. Customer service encompasses a wide range of responsibilities. for instance, if you tell someone you are going to be there at a specific time, you should arrive 15 minutes early and be prepared to encounter obstacles along the way, such as heavy traffic or an accident that causes you to be late. In the worst-case scenario, you will experience these delays,

however, if you have planned for them, you will be OK, and in the best-case scenario, you will arrive ahead of schedule.

Even if you already know where you are going, take a few moments to plan your route using Google Maps so that you can view real-time traffic information. Even when I know where I'm going, I still type the address into my Google Maps app on my iPhone, and it tells me the best route to take based on the time of day and the current traffic conditions so that I can plan my trip more efficiently.

When it comes to providing excellent customer service, one of the most essential lessons to learn is to never mislead or deceive clients by telling them things that are not entirely accurate or exaggerating the quality of products or services you offer. At the end of the day, you may give them a warm and fuzzy feeling as a result of what you told them, but as time passes, they will realize that wasn't correct

"If they could do it, then you could do it too."

information, and it

will be 10 times worse for you than if you just told them the truth up front. Your credibility is incredibly crucial, and if they lose your trust, you will not only lose them as a customer or client, but you will also lose any future referrals that you may have received from them.

Whether or not you put it on paper, if you tell someone you're going to do something, you should do it. It's as simple as that.

If you have made a mistake or promised someone something and then discovered that you cannot fulfill what you said, then it is best to just come clean and explain the situation to them. If you notice that the conversation is going in a negative direction at any point, you need to devise a strategy to turn things around. You should do this even if it costs you a small amount of money or time, because in the long run, it will cost you more to lose a good client and possibly lose referrals from new clients if you do not retain them.

Do you remember when I was talking about finding a balance between work and life? If you advertise that you are open during a given time range, you need to make sure that someone is there to answer the phone during that time. If you are promoting your business as being open at that hour, the worst thing you could do would be to not answer the phone when it rings. You can hire an answering service, but the problem is that the answering service will not be as good as you are at interacting with a potential new client. At that point, you might as well just send them to your voicemail and hope that they leave you a message and don't call your competitor instead.

It's true that there are answering services that do more than just collect messages, but at the end of the day, those services don't have nearly as much invested in a client or a possible new client as you do.

"If they could do it, then you could do it too."

If you truly are unable to answer the phone for some reason, you should send it to someone else that is as familiar with your company almost as well as you are and who can respond appropriately to most of the same questions that you can.

If you say you're open, even if you're in the middle of something like lunch or dinner or even out on a boat fishing, answer the phone, there is no gray area. It's possible that you find my manner of expression to be rude, but the point that I'm trying to make is significant. At the end of every job, you should ask your customers directly, "How do you think I did?" The answer to this question could determine whether you become successful. I asked each one of my customers, and I continue to ask them on a regular basis to be truthful with me and to let me know what they think. If they don't, I won't know what I'm doing right and what I'm doing wrong.

It is critical to have open lines of communication with one's customers before, during, and after the completion of a transaction. Maintain a database of all your customers, including their phone numbers, email addresses, and a detailed account of the work you accomplished for each one. I keep in touch with all my customers by using a database like excel; our interactions could be as infrequent as once every six months or once every year. You never know when they will require your assistance again or if they will have a friend or family member who could benefit from it. They will forget who you are just because life happens, so it is your job to stay in front of them without becoming overbearing. It is not necessary to get in touch with them more frequently than once every few months; typically, this can be accomplished by sending a postcard or an email.

When you are engaging in two-way communication with your customers, it is imperative that everything you send them, from your business cards to the automobile you drive, exudes an air of professionalism. You may not be able to afford a flashy vehicle for your company, but you should still

"If they could do it, then you could do it too."

make sure that it is clean and presentable because first impressions matter. This also applies to the way that you dress. If you run a service-based business, make sure that you and your employees wear uniforms that are clean and presentable and that do not have any rips in them. Make sure your hair is neat and that you are well groomed. It is important that you dress and present yourself appropriately as a professional in your field.

It is imperative that you give the impression that you have been engaged in this line of work for a considerable amount of time. Whenever you communicate with current or prospective customers, whether it be in person or remotely, you want to exude an air of experience. Do not attempt any short cuts on this.

When it comes to your customers, there is one more thing you need to remember. If you meet with them in person, you should listen more than you talk, unless you are describing the services you provide.

First and foremost, you need to understand what your customers are looking for. Learn about their circumstance, the problem they are experiencing, and the reason they turned to you in the first place. Not everyone is the same, once you have gathered all the details, you should go to the potential client and explain how you can or cannot assist them. Keep in mind what we discussed before and don't make more promises than you can keep. It is essential that you avoid making educated guesses when there are inquiries to which you do not have answers. Tell them that you will get back to them as soon as possible but that you need to do additional research first. Although a lot of people demand responses straight away, it is preferable to provide them with an accurate answer instead of coming to them with issues later.

Ask your client how they would like to be addressed and remember that so that when you talk to them again in the future, you can address them by how they wanted to be addressed. Example, you address

"If they could do it, then you could do it too."

someone by their first name, it gives the impression that you have a close relationship with them and that they can put their faith in you.

Yes, I am aware that you are probably asking yourself, "What if I'm not friends with them?" and I can assure you that I am aware of this. Therefore, you should try to become friends with them. I am not suggesting that you go to lunch or supper with them, but you should offer them your cell phone number. My mobile phone, has two different phone numbers set to ring. They both ring on the same phone. One of my phone lines is for my business, while the other is for my personal use. If you offer someone your cell phone number, they will feel a lot more at ease communicating with you. I'd even go so far as to save their phone number in your phone so that when they call, their name appears and you can respond by saying hello with their name; trust me, this will impress them even more. When you give someone your cell phone number, they get the impression that they might contact you at any time and that they are important to you. This is because they know that you always have your phone with you.

When you answer the phone at your place of business, you should always introduce yourself and state the name of your firm. Example: "I want to thank you for calling ABC Company. My name is [insert your name], and I'm wondering how I may assist you today." This is going to get you very far. Always be sure to check your e-mail, and I don't mean just once or twice a day on your mobile device. Check it consistently. I suggest that you enable push notifications on your mobile device so that, if an email pertaining to your company arrives, you will be notified immediately. Drop a quick note saying that you received their email and stating that you will get back to them as soon as possible.

You also have the option of setting up an automatic responder, which would state that your email has been received, a response will be sent as soon as possible, and we apologize for the delay.

"If they could do it, then you could do it too."

To reiterate, if you can answer phone do so, Therefore, let's conduct a fast review: don't make more promises than you can keep, answer the phone when it rings, perform what you say you're going to do, and maintain communication with your customers even after the task is done. Every customer should be treated as if they are the only one you have, regardless of the amount of money they are paying you, whether it is $5 or $5,000.

Jimmy Bitzas

"If they could do it, then you could do it too."

CHAPTER 8

Technology

Technology is a very essential topic when it comes to your business. The modern 24-hour news cycle contributes to the quick escalation of change in today's world. The introduction of new technologies that render previously existing businesses and services obsolete. If you really want to succeed in business, you must become comfortable with technology. This includes anything from marketing software to bookkeeping software and search engine optimization software.

You also need to consider what hardware you will need and how you will keep it up to date. When it comes to running a company, you probably don't know very many individuals who don't have a cellphone, especially if they work for themselves.

Make sure that you are using a carrier that has good coverage in your service area, even if you must pay a premium. The last thing you want to do is have dropped calls or talk to a potential new client and sound like you're in a tin can. Your mobile device must be able to maintain a healthy battery charge in addition to receiving emails and text messages. If your phone is unable to do any of these tasks, then you should consider upgrading to one that does.

Let's talk about the general software you may require. I inspect homes for clients. Because it is such a specialized field, I don't have many options when it comes to the software that I use during a home inspection, so I pay $30 a month to get access to it. I'm talking about some software that's going to make my life simpler, which will, in turn, help me strike a better balance between my personal and professional life.

You may recall that I mentioned previously in this book that if I could engage third-party organizations

"If they could do it, then you could do it too."

to take care of things for me, such as SEO and marketing, I would. I can appreciate the fact that, due to the high cost of some of those services, you may not be in a position financially to engage the services of a third-party company to handle them on your behalf. The good news is that there are many third-party software programs available, most of which charge a low price on a monthly basis that will direct you through the process of performing tasks such as search engine optimization (SEO). There are a few good ones available; the one that I use is called Semrush. There are several, so you should do your research to choose the one that is most suitable for you. I also propose that you take advantage of the hundreds of free resources that are currently available to help you kick-start your business. Some of the tools that are available from Google, such as Google Analytics and the Google keyword research tools, come highly recommended. If I were only selling products online only and not any kind of services, then yes, I would not use a scratch-built site, I would use a do-it-yourself website like Shopify because, in my opinion, they have mastered the online shopping experience for purchasing products only, and they have made it easy for you to set it up. However, if you are not selling a product online, I still recommend that you hire somebody to create your website from scratch.

The one thing I would not do myself is create my own website. I would look for a website developer then I would look over the website designer's portfolio before deciding about hiring them. One of the things that I do to find a website builder is go to the websites of my competitors and scroll all the way to the bottom. Sometimes it has the name of the website creator, and I give them a call if I like their design. The benefit of doing this is that they are familiar with your industry when it comes to website design. Because of this, you won't have to reinvent the wheel because they have already sorted out all the difficulties before creating your website. I cannot stress enough how important it is to ensure that your website is original and not a carbon copy of a

"If they could do it, then you could do it too."

competitor's. You are likely ahead of the curve because they have all the keywords, including the long-tail keywords that we discussed in the last section. Remember that you don't need to work as hard as you think; you just need to work wisely. Check to see that all the photographs are originals and that you own them all. Make sure you tell them that you need the website to be SEO friendly, and when you are producing the content for the website, make sure that it includes all your keywords as well as your long-tail keywords. A gas station is an example of a short-tail keyword; however, individuals may also search for "Gas station with car wash" when looking for "gas station." This is an example of a long-tail keyword. Therefore, you would include the words "gas station" and "car wash" in the content of your website. When it comes to technology, it is important to embrace it and use it. If your company demands the use of a computer, you should ensure that your computer is capable of handling it both today and in the future. You don't want your business to collapse just so you can save a few dollars on something that, in the long run, will end up costing you more time, money, and problems.

If you hire someone to handle your marketing, including SEO, make sure that you tell them that you do not want any black-hat tricks. A "black hat" trick is when someone tries to trick Google's algorithm so that they rank higher in the search engines. If you hire someone to handle your marketing, including SEO, and they do things they shouldn't do like black hat tricks is that you will eventually get caught, and if you get banned by Google, it will be a very big problem. I have seen people who got banned, and at the end of the day, they had to create a new company name, start over with reviews, and create a new Google business page. It is not worth it to try to beat the system in this way. Google is a lot smarter than them and knows all the tricks. A list of some items that Google likes and does not like is provided below for your perusal.

#1: One of the things that Google likes to see is that

"If they could do it, then you could do it too."

your website is compatible with mobile devices and tablets, in addition to obviously being compatible with computers. Because of this, you should make sure that your website looks good no matter what device a user is using to look at it.

#2 One of the things that irritates Google the most is when a website has a lot of links that all point to the same location. It's all about the user experience, so don't just pack your website with a bunch of keywords and jargon that doesn't make any sense. They want to see information that's original. Make sure that it is both instructive and informative.

#3: Ensure that your website has an effective site map. A site map functions similarly to a road map and assists Google in indexing all the pages on your website. Speak with your web designer about the site map that is currently hosted on your website.

#4. Load speed: Recall that we discussed this earlier; it is essential to Google, and when someone clicks on your website, it should load quickly. If it takes too long to load, you will be penalized for it, so make sure it doesn't take too long. The simplest method to avoid this is to make sure that your website does not load slowly by including a lot of photographs or videos. Even though they may look good at first, in the long run, they do more harm than good.

#5: Ensure that your website possesses an SSL certificate. If you look at the top toolbar of a website, you'll see HTTPS or an image of a little pad lock. This indicates that the website possesses a security certificate. If the website only has HTTP, then it does not. People feel a much greater sense of security when they visit a website that possesses an SSL certificate. These certificates are not very expensive, they are simple to set up, and Google will penalize you for not having one.

#6: The quality of the content on your website is very high. This topic has been discussed in the past, but I felt compelled to bring it up once more. Make sure that your content is not just original but also

"If they could do it, then you could do it too."

frequently updated and informative. Always keep in mind that Google is looking to improve its relationship with its users.

#7 Backlinks. Backlinks are links on websites that are not owned by you but that point to your website. These links are found on other websites. Check to see that the website in question is one that would benefit from having a link back to your own. Backlinks have the potential to be beneficial if they are built properly, but they can also be detrimental if they are not. As an illustration, given that I am a home inspector, I have included a link to my website on the websites of several construction companies' websites. Since they build houses and I inspect houses, it makes perfect sense to connect this way.

In the beginning, make use of everything at your disposal to spread the word about your company and the services it provides. Everything is helpful, whether you work with influencers, advertise on Google, use local media, or list your website in local directories.

"If they could do it, then you could do it too."

Conclusion

I could have written a much longer version of this book, and you undoubtedly noticed that I covered some of the same ground more than once. If you read carefully, you'll be able to identify those sections; it wasn't an oversight. I thought those points were significant enough that I wanted you to read them more than once so that you would remember them, but my entire goal was to convey one point, which was that if you want to become an entrepreneur and start your own business, you can do so. I wanted to make sure you understood that point. I am a firm believer that if it was possible for someone else to accomplish something, then it is possible for you to accomplish it as well, period.

Before you scoff at what I just said and roll your eyes, let me explain. I know that some jobs require a certain level of skill, money, education, and sometimes even physical traits.

"If they could do it, then you could do it too."

There are some who take the lead, and there are those who follow. You are taking the initial steps toward becoming a leader simply by reading books like this one. At the end of the day, you need to be a leader in order to be an entrepreneur.

That wraps up my motivational speech for today. Let's have a conversation about the things that you read and listened to in this book. You need to give a lot of consideration to the first question, which is whether you want to launch a company. You should also carefully consider each of the benefits and drawbacks that we discussed.

The important question you need to ask yourself is whether you are in the right frame of mind to take on this project. If you are not in the appropriate frame of mind, there is a good possibility that you will fail.

When starting a new business, it's important to choose a field you're interested in, do all the research we talked about, and wait to put your plans into action until you've come up with a good marketing campaign.

Take the time to give some consideration to the issues of work-life balance. Make sure that you put your time to the best possible use. You're familiar with the proverb that life is unfair, right? It's pretty much the same when it comes to business. Sometimes things are just not fair, and that's why one person succeeds in a business while another doesn't, even though they both work extremely hard. The problem is, you really don't need to work as hard as you can; rather, you need to work as smart as you can.

First, you should plan for everything, and then you should reevaluate what you just planned. It's like the adage that goes, "Measure twice, cut once." I simply wanted to briefly touch on a topic that comes up in conversation with me rather frequently. If I didn't go to college or obtain the appropriate training, is it possible for me to be successful as an entrepreneur? My response is as follows: College is not the right

"If they could do it, then you could do it too."

choice for everyone; in fact, most successful businesspeople I've encountered did not attend college. Furthermore, college does not always produce leaders.

At the end of the day, you are either a leader or a follower, and I know it sounds a little bit cruel, but in my opinion, it has been that way for a considerable amount of time. This does not mean that you are unable to become a leader; I have seen several instances when this has been accomplished.

If you have the determination, you are a leader, you plan things out, and you are astute regarding the situation. You are going to do well. You can learn certain things in college, but I really believe that the best way to learn is through experience in the real world.

You may not agree with everything that I stated, but I hope that you were able to take something away from this book. A lot of the ideas in this book are drawn from my own personal experiences. I would like to take this opportunity to convey my gratitude to you for allowing me to share my thoughts with you regarding the most effective strategies to run a successful business. I hope that all your future pursuits are successful and wish you the best.

www.ingramcontent.com/pod-product-compliance
Lightning Source LLC
Chambersburg PA
CBHW071421210526
45465CB00001B/481